BOY SCOUTS OF AMERICA
MERIT BADGE SERIES

AMERICAN LABOR

"Enhancing our youths' competitive edge through merit badges"

BOY SCOUTS OF AMERICA®

Requirements

1. Using resources available to you, learn about working people and work-related concerns. List and briefly describe or give examples of at least EIGHT concerns of American workers. These may include, but are not limited to, working conditions, workplace safety, hours, wages, seniority, job security, equal-opportunity employment and discrimination, guest workers, automation and technologies that replace workers, unemployment, layoffs, outsourcing, and employee benefits such as health care, child care, profit sharing, continuing education, and retirement benefits.

2. With your counselor's and parent's approval and permission, visit the office or attend a meeting of a local union, a central labor council, or an employee organization, or contact one of these organizations via the internet. Then do EACH of the following:

    a. Find out what the organization does.

    b. Share the list of issues and concerns you made for requirement 1. Ask the people you communicate with which issues are of greatest interest or concern to them and why.

    c. Draw a diagram showing how the organization is structured, from the local to the national level, if applicable.

3. Explain to your counselor what labor unions are, what they do, and what services they provide to members. In your discussion, show that you understand the concepts of labor, management, collective bargaining, negotiation, union shops, open shops, grievance procedures, mediation, arbitration, work stoppages, strikes, and lockouts.

4. Explain what is meant by the adversarial model of labor-management relations, compared with a cooperative-bargaining style.

5. Do ONE of the following:

   a. Develop a time line of significant events in the history of the American labor movement from the 1770s to the present.

   b. Prepare an exhibit, a scrapbook, or a computer presentation, such as a slide show, illustrating three major achievements of the American labor movement and how those achievements affect American workers.

   c. With your counselor's and parent's approval and permission, watch a movie that addresses organized labor in the United States. Afterward, discuss the movie with your counselor and explain what you learned.

   d. Read a biography (with your counselor's approval) of someone who has made a contribution to the American labor movement. Explain what contribution this person has made to the American labor movement.

6. Explain the term *globalization*. Discuss with your counselor some effects of globalization on the workforce in the United States. Explain how this global workforce fits into the economic system of this country.

7. Choose a labor issue of widespread interest to American workers—an issue in the news currently or known to you from your work on this merit badge. Before your counselor, or in writing, argue both sides of the issue, first taking management's side, then presenting labor's or the employee's point of view. In your presentation, summarize the basic rights and responsibilities of employers and employees, including union members and nonunion members.

8. Discuss with your counselor the different goals that may motivate the owners of a business, its stockholders, its customers, its employees, the employees' representatives, the community, and public officials. Explain why agreements and compromises are made and how they affect each group in achieving its goals.

9. Learn about opportunities in the field of labor relations. Choose one career in which you are interested and discuss with your counselor the major responsibilities of that position and the qualifications, education, and training such a position requires.

Contents

Introduction 7
Us and Them: The Struggles Between
  Labor and Management 9
The American Labor Force Today. 33
Conflicting Views in the Workplace 43
Labor-Management Relations. 49
Career Opportunities in Labor Relations 58
Labor-Related Resources 62

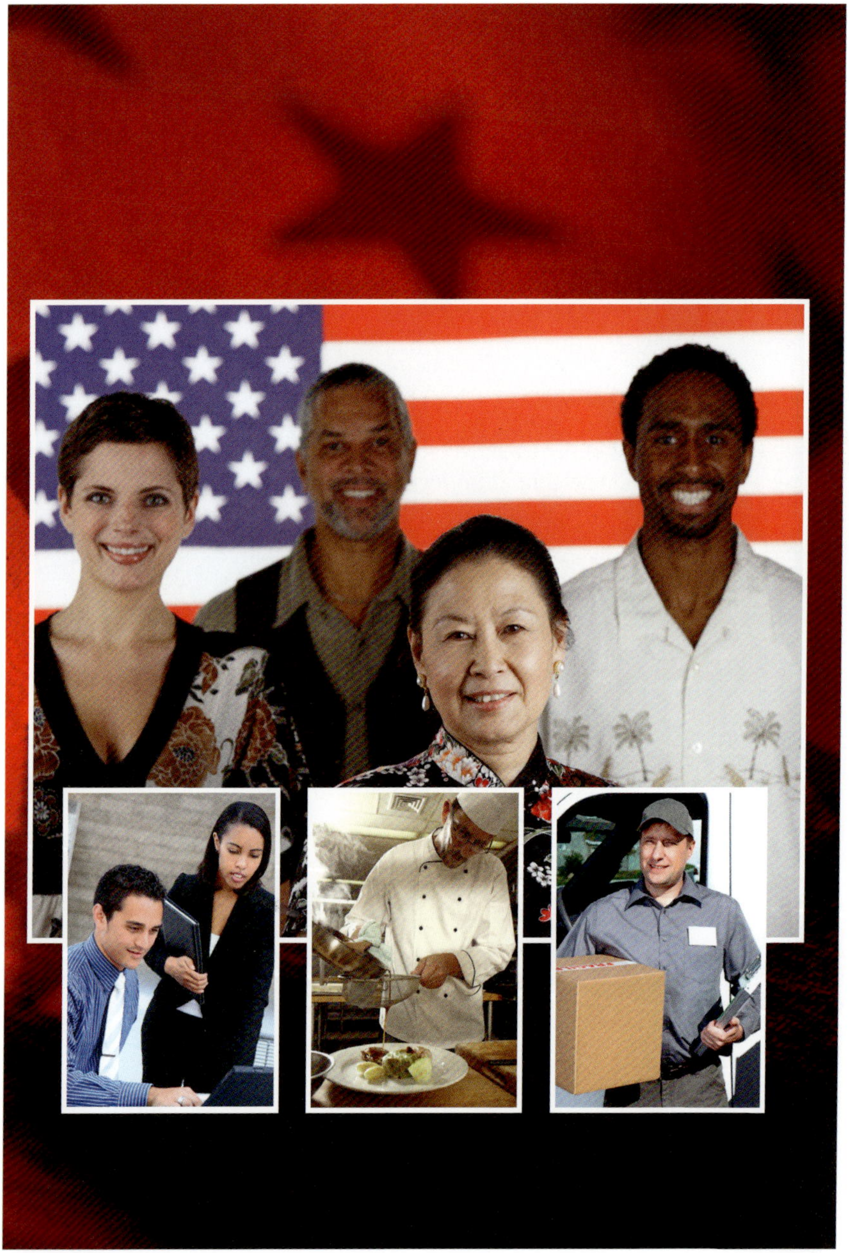

Introduction

The Declaration of Independence inspired many workers to demand their rights as people "created equal" to business owners. Just as the Colonists had united to name their *grievances* (complaints about wrongs suffered) against the British king, George III, and declare themselves independent of his control, American workers in specific trades came together to demand a *redress* (the setting right of unjust situations) of their grievances about low wages, long hours, and poor working conditions.

> You might be surprised to learn that the Boston Massacre in 1770 began as a labor dispute between an off-duty British soldier seeking a job to supplement his wage and a Colonial rope maker who resented having to compete with the soldier for scarce employment opportunities. Yet this event ignited a long fuse leading to the American Revolution, independence, and individual rights.

In time, these workers—particularly the "organized" labor force—demanded a voice in the workplace and *equity*, or a fair distribution of the benefits of economic prosperity. What they discovered is that democracy and capitalism, although they reinforce each other at many levels, often are at odds. The concept of *equal rights* clashes with *individual rights*. The *entrepreneur*, a person who starts a business and assumes the risks, wants to make a profit for his or her efforts. In fact, that person wants to make more profits than competitors.

What is "equal" about that? Should the people who work for the entrepreneur share the profits? These issues are at the core of the American labor movement.

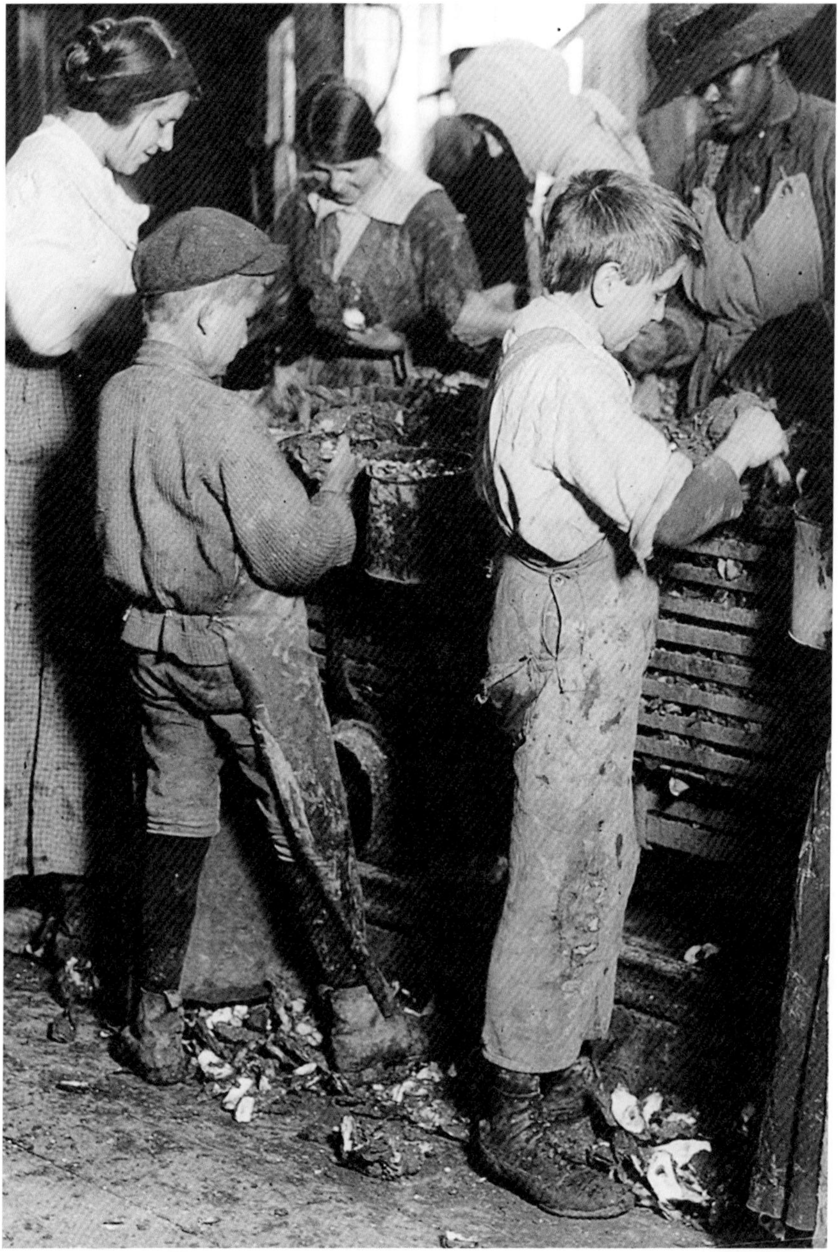

Us and Them: The Struggles Between Labor and Management

The economic development of the United States occurred in three stages. It began with settlers staking claims to land, then trying to raise crops and livestock to sustain their families. People worked to produce what they needed and could consume. In time, as trade developed, planters exported crops and artisans made items to sell.

The increased demand for products created an increased demand for labor—as well as an increased demand for higher profits. The invention of labor-saving machines, periods of prosperity and economic depressions, waves of immigration, and worker discontent led to critical changes in society. The majority of American workers were no longer independent and self-sufficient. Instead they had become employees, dependent on others for employment.

The pressure for ever-higher profits in a competitive economy resulted in management strategies to increase productivity by lowering wages and raising workday hours. Company owners spent money for machines instead of improvements to working conditions. Workers united to protest and protect their interests, including their health and safety. The labor movement began because of frustration with management and continues in the 21st century, as workers strive to maintain the gains they have made and work for resolutions to new conflicts.

> Factory workers often included children, who worked long hours under unsafe working conditions and were paid very little—sometimes nothing—for their work.

Agricultural Revolution and Slave Labor

When the founding fathers wrote the U.S. Constitution in 1787, they avoided addressing the issue of slavery in the document. The plantation system produced important cash crops for export, but it depended on the labor of enslaved African Americans.

In 1793, Eli Whitney invented the cotton gin, which removed cottonseeds quickly and cheaply. Now cotton could be grown profitably anywhere in the South, which encouraged planters to acquire more land by moving westward.

Through the 1850s, slaves produced most of the raw cotton for textile mills in Great Britain and in the northeastern part of the United States. Whether or not people supported the idea of slavery, they knew that slave labor was profitable.

Eli Whitney's cotton gin

Industrial Revolution and Free Labor

Industrial growth took off in the first half of the 19th century because the opportunities for trade expanded and new machines increased productivity. Canal systems and railroads allowed freight to move around the country more easily and cheaply. The invention of the steam printing press led to the widespread circulation of many different newspapers; the telegraph sent information instantly over long distances. The transportation and information networks knitted regional and national markets together.

Rural families started producing surplus crops and other goods for the market. They became less isolated and more aware of employment opportunities for their children. Young men often went west to buy and work their own land. Young women moved to towns and cities to work in the new textile mills and factories.

The rise of commercial agriculture and industries drastically changed the labor force. For centuries, most men learned a craft by working as an apprentice to a master craftsman, who owned his business. After years of training, the apprentice became a journeyman, or skilled craftsman. After more years of working for the master (and saving money), the journeyman started his own business as a master. The relationships were unequal, but the understanding that everyone had to spend time in training and the promise of becoming a master made the system work.

Iron worker creating steel, circa 1919

The factory system soon undermined the master-journeyman-apprentice arrangement. The availability of inexpensive and high-quality products shifted the demand to mass-produced items. Master craftsmen had to compete with mills and factories. Many furniture makers, shoemakers, hatters, and tailors hired more apprentices, changed work methods, and increased production. Those who could not compete lost their businesses and worked as journeymen for other masters or took jobs in factories.

Employers determined that they could break down expensive skilled work into simple tasks that could be done for a lower cost in a centralized workshop under supervision. This *division of labor* into small, specialized operations allowed the employer to replace skilled journeymen with semiskilled workers, some of whom were women and children.

Factory workers put in 12 hours a day, six days a week. Conditions in the factory and boarding houses where they lived seemed tolerable until the arrival of several million European immigrants during the mid- to late 1800s. These newcomers joined the ranks of the semiskilled employees, increasing the competition for a limited number of factory jobs and driving wages down. More factories opened, so company owners competed with each other while trying to protect profits.

By increasing production and lowering the piece rate, the employers effectively froze the workers' wages and increased their own profits. The workload of the average worker more than doubled, but only the owner benefited.

The hostility toward immigrants grew in different areas of the country during in the mid-1800s. A famine in China and the discovery of gold in California brought many Chinese

The dangerous working conditions factory workers endured for many years eventually led to laws and labor unions that helped protect workers.

12   AMERICAN LABOR

===== Us and Them: The Struggles Between Labor and Management

Employers cut costs by using several tactics.

1. **Speed-up**—Workers had to increase the rate at which the machines operated.
2. **Stretch-out**—Workers had to increase the number of machines they tended.
3. **Piece-rate reduction**—The employer lowered the price paid per piece produced.

people to the West Coast. By 1860, more than 35,000 Chinese immigrants worked in California mining camps. In 1848, the U.S. victory over Mexico in the U.S.-Mexican War resulted in the acquisition of land from Texas to California. Nearly 80,000 people, mostly of Spanish-Indian descent, would provide the low-paying labor to make agriculture, mining, and ranching profitable in that region. Native-born Americans resented having to compete for work with the people of Spanish-Indian descent. They also feared that the abolition of slavery would flood the labor force with freed slaves, threatening more jobs and driving wages even lower.

Native-born workers resented their employers' actions as well as the immigrants who were willing to work for less money and often took their jobs.

Thousands of Chinese immigrants helped build the transcontinental railroad during the 1860s.

AMERICAN LABOR   13

Birth of the Labor Movement

The labor movement began in the 18th century with local crafts organizations known as *benevolent societies*. These groups provided financial assistance to a worker or his family in case of debt, illness, or death. Later, journeymen in specific crafts united on a temporary basis to protest wage reductions and long workdays.

Eventually, different unions tried to win *recognition* from management to be the sole bargaining agent for all workers in a particular *bargaining unit*, or group. Some unions demanded *closed shops* where only union members were hired. Employers tried to avoid dealing with unions by hiring nonunion workers and appealing to the courts to declare unions illegal. Courts prosecuted the unions as "criminal conspiracies in restraint of trade." Later, the courts decided that unions were legal but challenged the methods unions used to make gains, such as strikes and boycotts.

---

agency shop. A workplace where nonunion employees of the bargaining unit (group covered by collective bargaining) must pay the union a sum equal to union dues as a condition of continuing employment.

closed shop. A workplace where only union members could be hired. Workers had to join the union before being employed. This practice was outlawed with the Labor-Management Relations Act of 1947.

open shop. A place of employment where workers are not required to join the union.

union shop. A workplace where every member of the bargaining unit must become a member after a specified amount of time.

A new social class emerged as more and more workers became wage earners. Unions organized for the economic benefit of the members and got involved in independent political activity. In the 1820s, political labor parties such as the Workingmen's Party brought attention to the social and economic problems of workers. Their efforts led to legislation that prohibited imprisonment for debt and established a 10-hour workday for women and children. They also laid the groundwork for the establishment of the free public school system.

===== Us and Them: The Struggles Between Labor and Management

Workers tried to organize local unions of different crafts into citywide groups called *city central groups,* or *trades unions.* In the second half of the 19th century, they concentrated on forming national unions of workers in the same crafts. Two important federations of national unions—with different agendas—developed after the Civil War.

> "An injury to one is an injury to all."
> —the slogan for the Knights of Labor

The Noble and Holy Knights of Labor, organized in 1869 as a secret society of tailors, went public in 1879. Led by **Terence V. Powderly,** the *inclusive union* accepted workers of all skill levels and trades (except lawyers, politicians, and liquor dealers). The union encouraged men and women of all races and national origins to become members. Powderly's broad social vision, which focused on reforms and political issues, alienated many members who wanted the leader to concentrate on economic concerns.

In 1886, skilled workers in craft unions organized the American Federation of Labor. **Samuel Gompers,** the leader of this loose confederation of *autonomous* (self-ruling) unions, ran the AFL as a *business union,* focusing on bread-and-butter issues such as securing better wages and working conditions and mandating the eight-hour workday.

Key leaders in the labor movement are mentioned in **bold print** in this pamphlet. To learn more about any one of them, read one of the biographies listed in the resources section.

> "To be free, the workers must have choice. To have choice, they must retain in their own hands the right to determine under what conditions they will work."
> —*Samuel Gompers*

AMERICAN LABOR   15

Us and Them: The Struggles Between Labor and Management

> Union members call people who cross picket lines and work during a strike "scabs."

While workers organized large national labor organizations, industrialists merged with competitors to create huge, powerful companies. Big business fought union efforts to have any influence in the workplace. Management used the court injunction, private armies, and federal troops to put down labor activity. Employers also contracted with prisons to hire convicts as strikebreakers. Trade unionism grew in fits and starts in response to the success or failure of strikes, boom-and-bust business cycles, and union militancy.

The Labor Movement in the 20th Century

Labor leaders promoted the ideas of union *solidarity* (a spirit of unity based on common interests) and democracy in the workplace. However, deep-rooted prejudice and fear often exerted a stronger influence on union members than idealism. High unemployment and competition for jobs during economic depressions contributed to the following problems:

- Discrimination against foreign-born workers, minorities, and women
- Splits between skilled and unskilled workers
- Power struggles between supporters of business unionism and radical labor activists such as members of the Socialist Party and the Communist Party

Labor Day

For more than 100 years, the first Monday in September has been designated Labor Day, a holiday that recognizes the contributions of workers to the economic strength and social well-being of the United States. The first Labor Day celebration was held on September 5, 1882, in New York City and was organized by the Central Labor Union. Highlights of the celebration included a parade attended by about 10,000 workers, picnics, concerts, and speeches.

As the labor movement gained ground, Labor Day celebrations grew in popularity. In 1894, Congress passed a bill that made Labor Day a national holiday. Early Labor Day celebrations followed the model of the first Labor Day and usually featured parades, family entertainment, and speeches. Today, many people take the victories of the labor movement for granted, but government offices, banks, and many private businesses still close in recognition of the holiday, giving workers a chance to enjoy a day off from their labors.

Us and Them: The Struggles Between Labor and Management

The disunity within the rank and file weakened the unions and allowed *racketeers* to infiltrate and corrupt some labor organizations. Employers publicized charges of union corruption to turn public opinion against labor's organizing efforts.

As a result of worker unrest, new unions formed. In 1900, the International Ladies' Garment Workers' Union (ILGWU) formed in response to the horrible conditions in *sweatshops*—workplaces where employees labored for long hours and low wages in unsanitary and dangerous conditions. A strike in 1909 by 20,000 (mostly women) members resulted in a compromise with manufacturers that provided for preferential hiring of union members and prohibited employers from contracting with outside workers to do *homework*—sewing tasks performed at home at the worker's expense.

In 1911, the Triangle Shirtwaist Company fire in New York City's garment district killed 146 women workers. The women were unable to escape because the factory doors were locked. In the aftermath of the fire, labor unions and other social and political groups rallied to protest the conditions that had led to the tragedy.

Us and Them: The Struggles Between Labor and Management

In 1905, *socialists* and other workers formed a radical labor organization, the Industrial Workers of the World. The goal of the IWW was to create One Big Union—a single union for all workers—and overthrow the industrialists. The IWW, led by **William D. "Big Bill" Haywood,** used controversial tactics, but it was one of the few unions to champion the rights of immigrant workers in the West. The IWW opposed U.S. participation in World War I for ethical and political reasons and encouraged strikes to disrupt the war effort. As a result, Haywood was convicted of treasonous crimes. After a brief

> *Communism* advocates the collective ownership and distribution of goods and does not recognize the concept of private property. In 1848, **Karl Marx** and **Friedrich Engels** defined the concepts of this theory in *The Communist Manifesto.* Marx believed that throughout history social classes have struggled for control of labor and production. He thought that business owners oppressed the workers and predicted that the laborers would revolt and overthrow the capitalists.

In 1925, *A. Philip Randolph,* a labor leader and civil rights activist, organized African American railroad employees (excluded from most railroad unions) into the Brotherhood of Sleeping Car Porters. He crusaded for higher wages and the improvement of working conditions for all workers.

Educator and advocate of democracy, freedom, and civil rights, *Albert Shanker* served as president of the American Federation of Teachers for 23 years, until his death in 1997. During his tenure at the AFT, Shanker succeeded in raising national academic standards and improving classroom teaching.

18   AMERICAN LABOR

stint in prison, he fled the United States to lend his support to the socialist revolution in Russia.

The AFL's failure to organize the semiskilled and unskilled workers in the mass production industries provoked **John L. Lewis,** president of the United Mine Workers of America, and seven other AFL union leaders in 1935 to organize the Committee for Industrial Organization. The AFL expelled the CIO unions, which then formed a permanent independent federation renamed the Congress of Industrial Organizations. The CIO showed more militancy against employers, including the rarely used tactic of a sit-down strike, thus winning union recognition in unorganized industries and the right to engage in collective bargaining.

Union membership declined sharply during the 1920s and into the early 1930s, much of it due to extreme antiunion action by employers, restrictive court rulings, and business-oriented legislation of the era. Workers became desperate for change in the early 1930s and began organizing and holding wildcat strikes, often causing disruption in production. In an attempt to revitalize the economy and bring peace to the workforce, President Franklin Delano Roosevelt offered the American people a New Deal and pushed through social-reform programs and pro-labor legislation to help the working class. Congress passed the National Labor Relations Act, giving private sector workers the right to organize and bargain collectively. The law states, "It is declared to be the policy of the United States ... by encouraging the practice and procedure of collective bargaining and by protecting the exercise by workers of full freedom of association, self-organization, and designation of representatives of their own choosing, for the purpose of negotiating the terms and conditions of their employment or other mutual aid or protection." Reforms included unemployment insurance and Social Security, which required workers and employers to pay a tax to the federal government in order to provide a pension to retired employees.

Thanks to favorable labor laws and successful organizing drives, union membership rapidly increased. Roosevelt recognized labor's growing influence and appointed many labor representatives to federal agencies. In return, the unions pledged not to strike while the country was at war. Most unions honored the pledge and enjoyed a high rate of employment.

When the war ended in 1945, unions went on strike. They brought out all the grievances they had shelved during the war

Rosie the Riveter

During World War II, the female labor force grew by more than 5 million workers as women stepped into jobs vacated by the men who had gone to fight. The women joined unions, proved they could build planes and automobiles as well as men, and demanded equal pay for equal work.

and demanded their share of the country's economic prosperity. Labor scored many successes, which caused concern in business and government that the unions were becoming too powerful. New legislation, such as the Labor-Management Relations Act, reversed many of labor's gains from Roosevelt's New Deal.

The American Federation of Labor, led by **George Meany,** and the Congress of Industrial Organizations, led by **Walter Reuther,** recognized that support for labor was changing. The two rival organizations decided to merge to protect union strength. In 1955, George Meany became the first president of the AFL-CIO.

The new organization set about ousting racketeers from the unions. A few unions were expelled because of corruption. The negative publicity fueled an effort to keep unions out of business and gave additional support to state right-to-work laws, which prohibit closed shops.

Despite public opinion and new labor laws, unions negotiated much higher wages for their members than those of nonunion workers as well as a variety of employer-paid fringe benefits. The economy prospered. Unions, business, and the government developed a *social compact*—an unspoken agreement to work with each other as long as everyone was making money.

The economy sputtered during the 1970s, and millions of workers lost high-paying industrial jobs. The least-skilled and least-educated workers were the first to go. Many of these people found work in low-paying service jobs. Membership in those unions that represented the big manufacturers decreased but increased in unions representing service industries and government workers. The Industrial Revolution had ended.

> On April 4, 1968, Martin Luther King Jr. was assassinated in Memphis, Tennessee, where he had come to support a sanitation workers' strike.

Racketeering is making money through illegal activities, such as extorting money for providing "protection."

AMERICAN LABOR 21

Us and Them: The Struggles Between Labor and Management

The Social Compact
Post–World War II to 1960s

The federal government developed a foreign policy that benefited U.S. business interests. In turn, companies tolerated government "meddling"—the result of increased regulating powers.

BUSINESS

GOVERNMENT

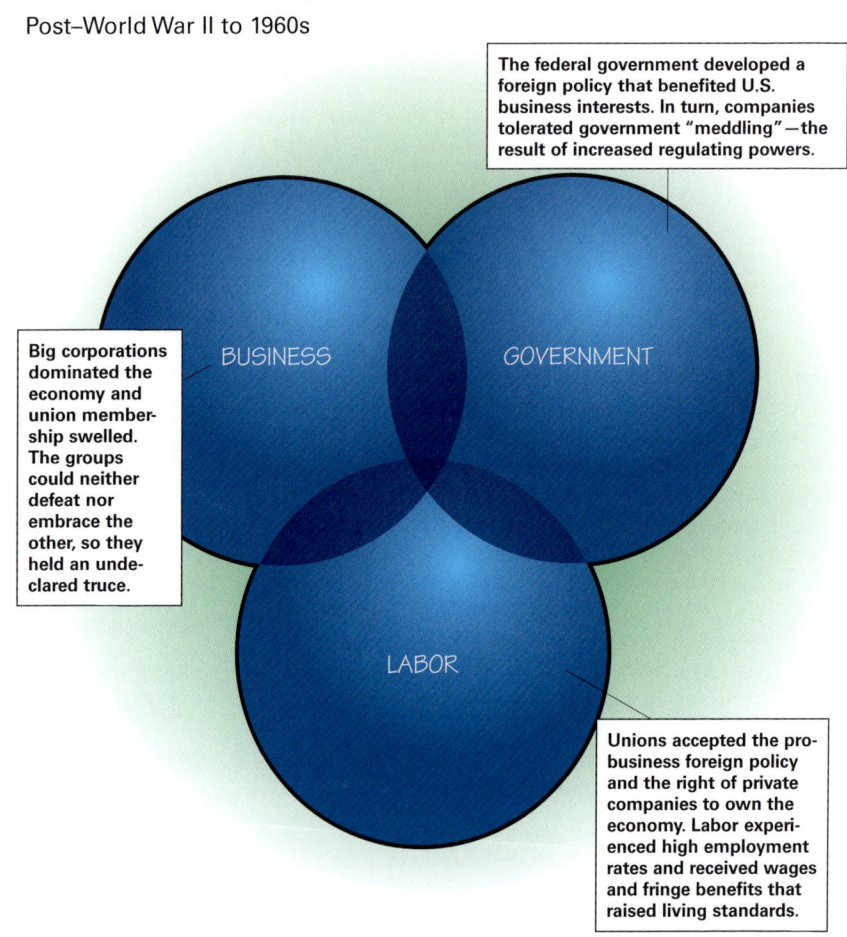

LABOR

Big corporations dominated the economy and union membership swelled. The groups could neither defeat nor embrace the other, so they held an undeclared truce.

Unions accepted the pro-business foreign policy and the right of private companies to own the economy. Labor experienced high employment rates and received wages and fringe benefits that raised living standards.

The civil rights movement in the 1960s raised the issue of discrimination and challenged the unions' predominantly white male leadership. In 1963, A. Philip Randolph (the labor activist who had organized the Brotherhood of Sleeping Car Porters) led the March on Washington for Jobs and Freedom, where he and 250,000 people heard Dr. Martin Luther King Jr. give his "I Have a Dream" speech.

Labor Rights as Human Rights

The rights of workers are also found in international documents such as the Universal Declaration of Human Rights that was proclaimed by the United Nations General Assembly in 1948 and states "Everyone has the right to form and to join trade unions for the protection of [their] interests."

A number of other international documents, such as the U.N.'s International Covenant on Civil and Political Rights and International Covenant on Economic, Social, and Political Rights, and, most specifically, the International Labor Organization's Conventions Nos. 87 (Freedom of Association and Protection of the Right to Organize) and 98 (Right to Organize and Collective Bargaining), articulate labor rights as basic human rights.

The American labor movement has long been a champion of promoting democracy and opposing dictatorships. Its fight against the efforts of communists to take control of unions in Europe following World War II helped the Marshall Plan succeed and democracy flourish in war-torn countries. It also fought authoritarian dictators whose goal was to eliminate unions as an independent voice of workers in many nations.

Information Revolution and Global Labor

During the 1980s and 1990s, the semiconductor and microchip changed everything. With personal computers, global communications satellites, and the internet, people could instantly transfer information, ideas, and money around the world. Many jobs became available for people who understood information technology. Top executives and highly skilled IT workers made a lot of money. However, many industrial jobs for skilled and educated people were lost. These workers were forced to compete with the unskilled for low-paying service jobs.

Manufacturing companies restructured, laying off employees who had earned enough to support a family on one salary. Middle management and lower-level workers who had little hope of getting their jobs back scrambled for work as millions of women entered the labor force to help maintain family incomes.

Where the Jobs Are . . . And Were*

2014		2004	
Walmart	1,400,000	Walmart	1,200,000
U.S. Postal Service	491,017	McDonald's	418,000
International Business Machines (IBM)	431,212	United Parcel Service	355,000
Kroger	375,000	Ford Motor Company	327,500
Target	366,000	General Motors	325,000

*This table compares total employment at the five largest U.S. companies based on rankings from *Fortune* magazine (2004) and S&P Capital IQ (2014).

Globalization

For more than 200 years, the United States participated in an international economy. Trade took place between nations, and governments set the rules. Commerce in the 21st century involves a global economy. Corporations, investment bankers, and traders treat the world as one big market. Global business is changing so rapidly that democratic governments are losing their ability to protect national interests and their labor force.

Multinational corporations (companies that operate in different countries) use technology to create *comparative advantage*, the economic principle that each nation should produce what it makes best and most cheaply and then trade those goods with another nation for what that nation makes best and most cheaply. Multinational corporations set up factories in several countries to make parts or components wherever the costs are lowest, union control is weakest, labor laws are most relaxed, and tax rates are most advantageous. Using computers and communications satellites, the companies send manufacturing specifications to plants around the world. Then they ship the parts to another country for assembly.

"Made in America" doesn't mean what it once did. An American car has parts made all over the world; many Japanese cars are assembled in the United States. Much of world trade today is not between countries, but between different parts of global companies.

Us and Them: The Struggles Between Labor and Management

The Social Compact . . . Unlinked
21st Century

- GLOBAL MARKET
- MULTINATIONAL COMPANIES
- U.S. GOVERNMENT
- U.S. LABOR & OUTSOURCE SATELLITES

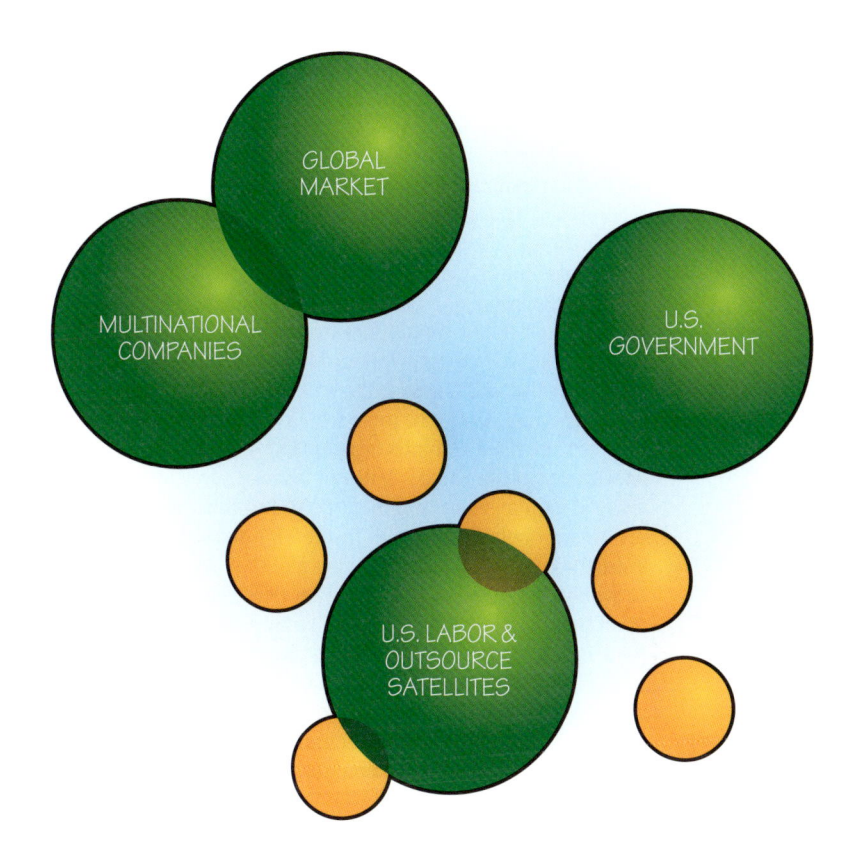

Outsourcing is the practice of subcontracting jobs to outside workers, especially to foreign or nonunion companies and individuals. This practice often cuts costs because the company does not pay benefits to the outside workers. Outsourcing has produced a new group of temporary and part-time employees, including freelancers, contract laborers, and consultants, who work without benefits on a by-project basis.

AMERICAN LABOR

Corporations are sending manufacturing jobs and service jobs offshore. Jobs in data entry, customer service, claims processing, telemarketing, software engineering, and business analysis are some examples of the positions that have moved overseas.

Computerized trading and instant access to current information about foreign currencies allow a global financial market to operate day and night around the world. Traders invest not only in money, but also in companies worldwide. They want a maximum return on their investments, so they look for businesses that use *best practices,* that is, the most economical, efficient, and profitable way to do or produce something. Companies that keep costs down and productivity up generate the biggest profits and get the traders' money. Corporations seeking investment capital have to make hard decisions about restructuring the company, cutting wages and benefits, laying off employees, and outsourcing or eliminating positions.

The American labor force feels threatened. Many workers believe they have lost jobs to *guest workers,* nonimmigrants admitted into the United States on special visas to work for specific employers for a limited period of time. Guest workers are particularly prevalent in the high-tech and agricultural industries. American workers also feel that they have lost jobs to workers in Third World countries (less economically developed nations in Africa, Asia, and Latin America) who will work for a much lower wage. Some Americans believe it is difficult to compete without giving back gains the labor movement has made. What frustrates many American workers is that some workers in the Third World (including children and convicts) labor long hours in terrible conditions for low wages—the same conditions that unions fought to change.

=== Us and Them: The Struggles Between Labor and Management

Guest Workers and Visas

Before guest worker visas are issued, employers interested in hiring guest workers must prove that a labor shortage exists; that foreign-born workers would not be taking jobs from Americans; and that the guest workers would be paid prevailing rates (average wages paid for a specific job in a geographical area or industry). Critics of the visa program claim that the labor shortage does not exist, that guest workers are paid less than the prevailing rate (which drives American wages lower), and that temporary jobs become permanent once the guest worker gets a *green card,* an identity card stating that the foreign worker has permanent resident status in the United States.

US AND THEM: THE STRUGGLES BETWEEN LABOR AND MANAGEMENT

Now Showing: Organized Labor in the United States

Clashes between workers and employers—often brutal—have been depicted in movies and in television documentaries. Many films are accounts of violent strikes, racketeering within unions, robber barons and corporate greed, plant closings, mysterious deaths of labor leaders and whistle-blowers, and union activity in textile mills, coal mines, and other industries. Whether fictionalized or not, these stories often reflect working-class history: the immigrant experience in the United States, extended periods of unemployment, low wages and long hours, civil rights and labor struggles, class-gender-race wars, and radical politics.

Generally, workers are portrayed as the good guys and management as the bad guys. That sets up dramatic plots—the powerless against the powerful, the little guy versus the big guy—but when viewing such a film, consider the issues from all sides. Were the issues presented fairly, or has an obvious pro-labor or antilabor perspective been portrayed?

You can find labor-themed films at video rental stores, public and university libraries, or at specific unions. The book *Working Stiffs, Union Maids, Reds, and Riffraff: An Expanded Guide to Films About Labor* (see resources section) provides reviews of 350 films that explore labor issues.

Famous Strikes

1877: The Baltimore & Ohio Railroad slashed wages and touched off a railroad strike that spread coast to coast. This uprising was the first industrywide strike and the first time a U.S. president called in federal troops to protect the interests of big business. Workers in other industries staged sympathy strikes in support of the railroad workers. By the time the strike was put down, 100 people were dead. The railroad strike polarized the social classes and forced Americans to side either with labor or with management. The strike also led to a new unity among workers and a revitalization of the labor movement.

1894: The American Railway Union called a strike against the Pullman Palace Car Company because **George Pullman,** owner of the railroad passenger car company, kept raising rents in his *company town* while reducing wages. (A company town is a community whose economy is dominated by one employer. The company owned all the land, buildings, houses, and stores.) Pullman closed his plants, so the union authorized a boycott. No ARU member would work on any train that included Pullman cars. The railroad companies refused to detach the cars, so the boycott became a general strike, which resulted in the shutting down of 11 railroad lines. For the first time, a federal court issued an *injunction,* or order to stop, on the basis that the strike "damaged interstate commerce and was a criminal conspiracy to obstruct postal service." President Grover Cleveland sent federal troops to enforce the court order. **Eugene V. Debs,** the leader of the ARU, ignored the injunction and was jailed for six months. The use of the injunction became management's major weapon against labor for the next 40 years.

George Pullman

1902: Anthracite coal miners who were members of the United Mine Workers called a strike against coal companies that lasted more than five months. President Theodore Roosevelt ordered arbitration, which ended in a compromise that increased wages. This was the first time a U.S. president intervened as a neutral third party to end a strike.

1936: The United Rubber Workers called a strike against the Goodyear Tire and Rubber Company in Akron, Ohio, after the company announced layoffs. This strike was important for several reasons:

- It was the first major labor conflict to use the sit-down strike as a tactic.
- It was the first strike by a union belonging to the newly formed Committee for Industrial Organization.
- It combined efforts by rank-and-file activists with support from Akron's central labor council and CIO headquarters.

1936–37: United Automobile Workers of America staged sit-down strikes against General Motors and then Chrysler. The strikes ended months later after the auto companies recognized the UAW as the sole bargaining agent for all employees.

1945–46: A wave of militant and successful strikes in as many as 44 states by the United Automobile Workers; United Electrical, Radio, and Machine Workers; and the United Steelworkers Union showed that American labor wanted its share of postwar prosperity. The UAW strike against General Motors was the first, largest, and longest postwar strike. For the first time, a union demanded that the company increase wages without passing on the cost to consumers. General Motors increased the autoworkers' wages but refused to negotiate on the prices of products. Two years later, the UAW did get the first cost-of-living escalator clause, which guaranteed that some pay increases would keep pace with rises in consumer prices.

1965: To help striking Filipino grape workers, **Cesar Chavez**—leader of the National Farm Workers Association (later to become the United Farm Workers)—called for a national grape boycott. The grassroots organizing effort led to a union contract with the growers that gave workers increased pay, employer-funded health care, housing, job-training programs, and union hiring halls. It also established a ban on the use of toxic pesticides such as DDT.

1960s–70s: Although strikes by public-sector employees were generally outlawed, many occurred as teachers, hospital and sanitation workers, and firefighters went on strike to win union recognition and collective-bargaining rights. In 1970, New York postal workers started what became the first national walkout (strike) by federal employees. Their wildcat strike for higher pay spread to other cities, despite federal injunctions. President Richard Nixon called in the National Guard to move the mail. The strike ended when the government agreed to negotiate substantial pay increases for the postal workers.

1981: The Professional Air Traffic Controllers Organization had complained for years that air traffic controllers suffered from stress because of a lack of staff and equipment to keep up with increased flight traffic. When they illegally went out on strike, President Ronald Reagan immediately warned the controllers to return to work or lose their jobs. When strikers did not return, he dismissed them. Within a month, replacement controllers were able to restore 75 percent of air service. Reagan's response signaled a new antilabor position.

1997: The International Brotherhood of Teamsters struck United Parcel Service to protest the company's strategy to subcontract work to non-union and part-time employees. A 15-day strike ended with a victory for the Teamsters when a federally mediated agreement forced UPS to create 10,000 new full-time jobs.

More than 180,000 Teamsters went on strike in 1997 to win concessions from UPS.

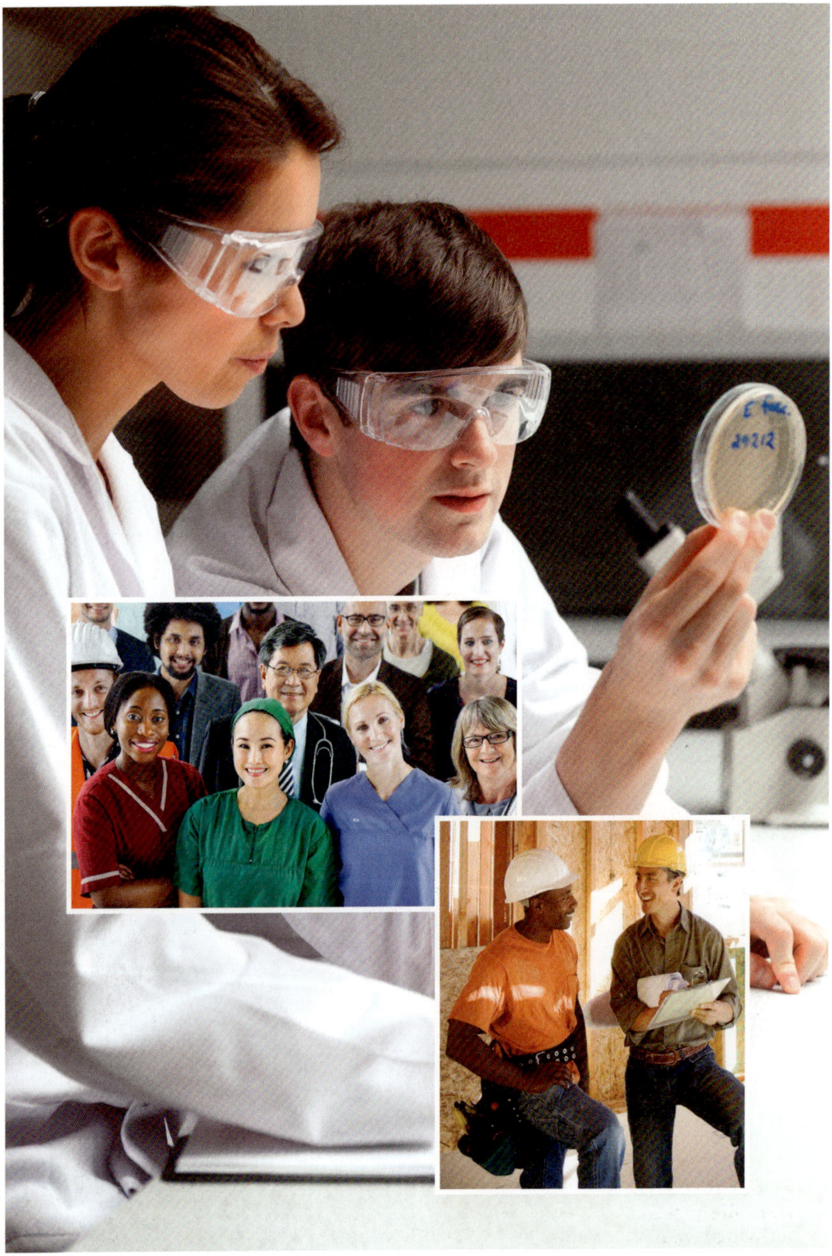

The American Labor Force Today

The American civilian labor force includes employed and unemployed people over 16 years old, except those in prisons, mental-health institutions, and nursing homes and people serving on active duty in the military. *Blue-collar workers* generally perform manual or physical work in construction, manufacturing, transportation, agricultural, and service industries. *White-collar employees* usually work in offices and schools and are not required to do heavy physical labor. Their occupations range from professional, technical, and managerial to clerical and sales positions.

Certain crafts such as electrical work and tool and die making demand a high level of skill and years of experience. Many professional and technical occupations require advanced levels of education. Other positions require little or no skill and just days or weeks of training.

Many welders attend a vocational school or community college to learn their trade and then receive further on-the-job training.

> Craft unions provide training to their members based on the model of medieval craft guilds. A trainee begins as an apprentice, learning a trade at a union-sponsored school and acting as an assistant on the job. After successfully completing a training period of four or more years, the apprentice becomes a fully qualified skilled worker, or journeyman.

The labor force serves two distinct parts of the nation's economy: the *private sector* and the *public sector*. The private sector refers to the aspects of the economy that are under the control of individuals and privately owned businesses. The public sector is under the control of the federal, state, or local governments.

Another way to analyze the workforce is in terms of *unorganized* versus *organized* labor. In unorganized labor situations, the individual employee addresses problems one-on-one with his or her supervisor and the managerial chain of command. In organized labor, a recognized group of workers deals with management as a collective body with one voice. Organized workers believe that all employees would benefit from belonging to a labor group. In fact, one of the main goals of unions is to organize the unorganized.

Labor Unions

A labor union is an association of workers in a specific craft or industry, with the main purpose of representing those workers in negotiations (collective bargaining) about wages, hours, and working conditions with the employer. Unions take different forms.

- *Craft unions* are horizontal. Members are skilled workers who perform one trade only, such as bricklayers, plumbers, screen actors, or airline pilots.

- *Industrial unions* are vertical. Members are skilled and unskilled workers in all trades within a single industry, such as the automobile, textile, or rubber industry.

Independent unions are craft or industrial unions that are not affiliated with the AFL-CIO, such as those that represent Major League Baseball players and certain groups of teachers.

The American Labor Force Today

More than half of the airline pilots in the United States are union members.

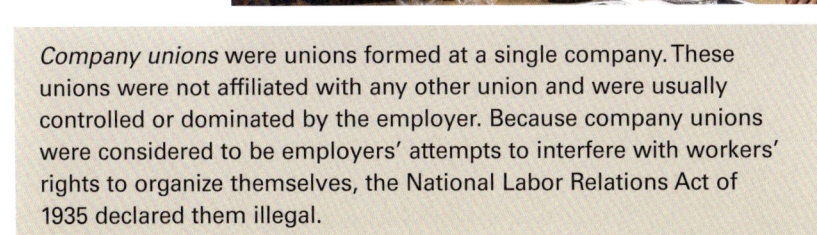

Company unions were unions formed at a single company. These unions were not affiliated with any other union and were usually controlled or dominated by the employer. Because company unions were considered to be employers' attempts to interfere with workers' rights to organize themselves, the National Labor Relations Act of 1935 declared them illegal.

THE AMERICAN LABOR FORCE TODAY

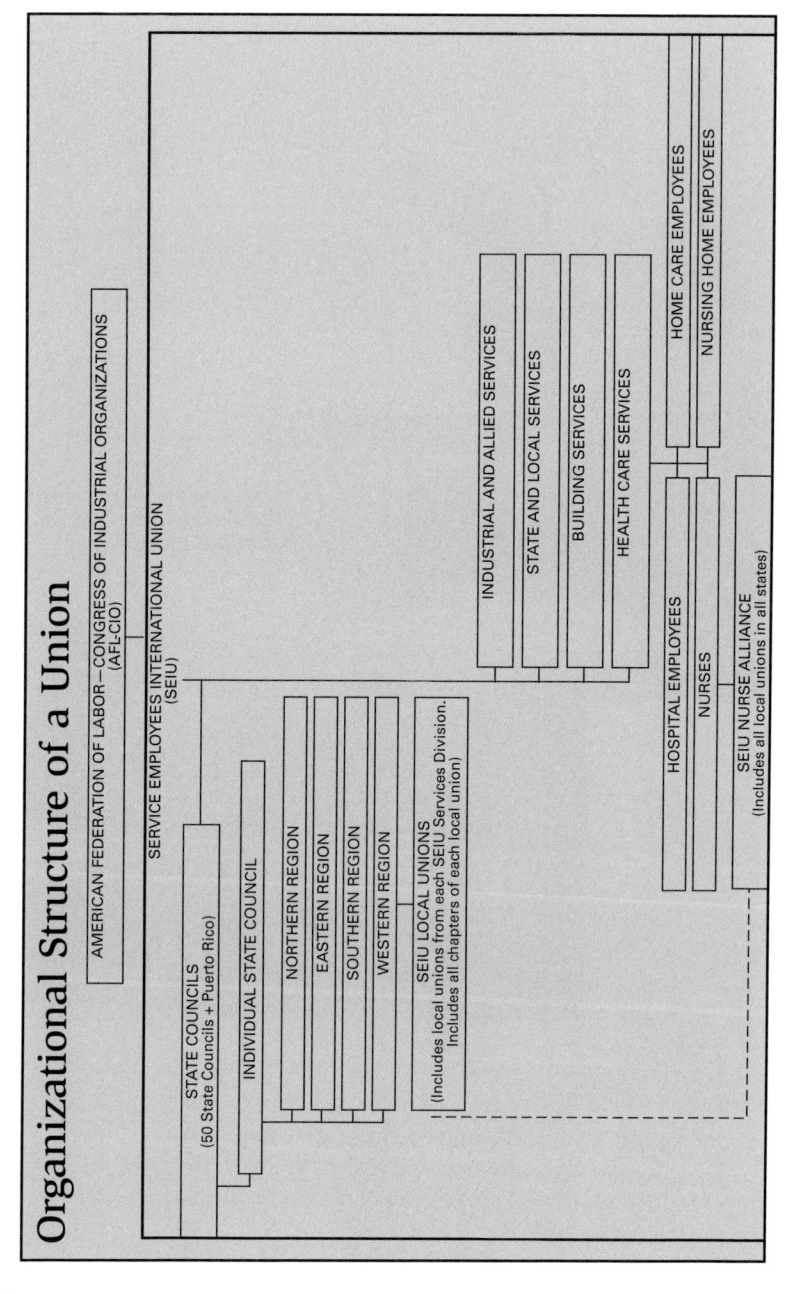

Organizational Structure of a Union

- AMERICAN FEDERATION OF LABOR—CONGRESS OF INDUSTRIAL ORGANIZATIONS (AFL-CIO)
  - SERVICE EMPLOYEES INTERNATIONAL UNION (SEIU)
    - STATE COUNCILS (50 State Councils + Puerto Rico)
      - INDIVIDUAL STATE COUNCIL
        - NORTHERN REGION
        - EASTERN REGION
        - SOUTHERN REGION
        - WESTERN REGION
    - SEIU LOCAL UNIONS (Includes local unions from each SEIU Services Division. Includes all chapters of each local union)
    - INDUSTRIAL AND ALLIED SERVICES
    - STATE AND LOCAL SERVICES
    - BUILDING SERVICES
    - HEALTH CARE SERVICES
      - HOSPITAL EMPLOYEES
      - NURSES
      - HOME CARE EMPLOYEES
      - NURSING HOME EMPLOYEES
    - SEIU NURSE ALLIANCE (Includes all local unions in all states)

36 AMERICAN LABOR

> The *local* union represents all union members in a specific workplace or all members of a craft union in a particular geographical area. It is the basic block in a union's structure. Unions may be local, national, or international organizations.

Unionization

If employees in a company decide they want union representation, they sign a petition, which is then sent to the National Labor Relations Board in Washington, D.C. If the Board certifies that there is enough interest to form a union, it authorizes a secret ballot election to take place in the workplace after a 60-day waiting period.

Many workers think the waiting period is unfair because it gives employers a chance to engage in antiunion activities that undercut the organizing efforts and elections. Today labor unions are promoting legislation that would require the NLRB to certify the formation of a union (without a waiting period and election) when a majority of employees have signed authorization cards or petitions to form a union.

Union Membership

As the nature of the U.S. economy has changed, union membership has changed, too. More people belonged to unions (as a percentage of the labor force) when industry powered the economy. In the past 50 years, however, union membership has dropped steadily as the economy has shifted from manufacturing to service industries. Many older members of traditional unions such as the United Automobile Workers and United Mine Workers of America have retired or lost their jobs to *downsizing*—laying off workers and reducing the workforce to cut costs.

The American Labor Force Today

In 2014, only 6.6 percent of private-sector employees belonged to a union compared with 35.7 percent of public-sector workers. The groups with the highest unionization rates are workers in education, training, library, and protective services including police officers, firefighters, and security guards. Four in 10 workers in each of these groups belong to a union.

The following are some of the reasons union membership has increased or decreased at various times in history:

- Economic cycles of prosperity or depression
- High employment or unemployment rates
- Government intervention such as injunctions
- National immigration trends and policies
- Pro-labor or antilabor legislation
- Employers' hostility toward unions
- Strike victories or failures
- Cases of corruption and racketeering
- Successful outcomes in collective-bargaining sessions
- Public perception that unions are special-interest groups

In the 21st century, unions are trying to find ways to adapt to changes in the economy, political environment, workforce, and labor-management relationship and to revitalize the labor movement.

═══════ THE AMERICAN LABOR FORCE TODAY

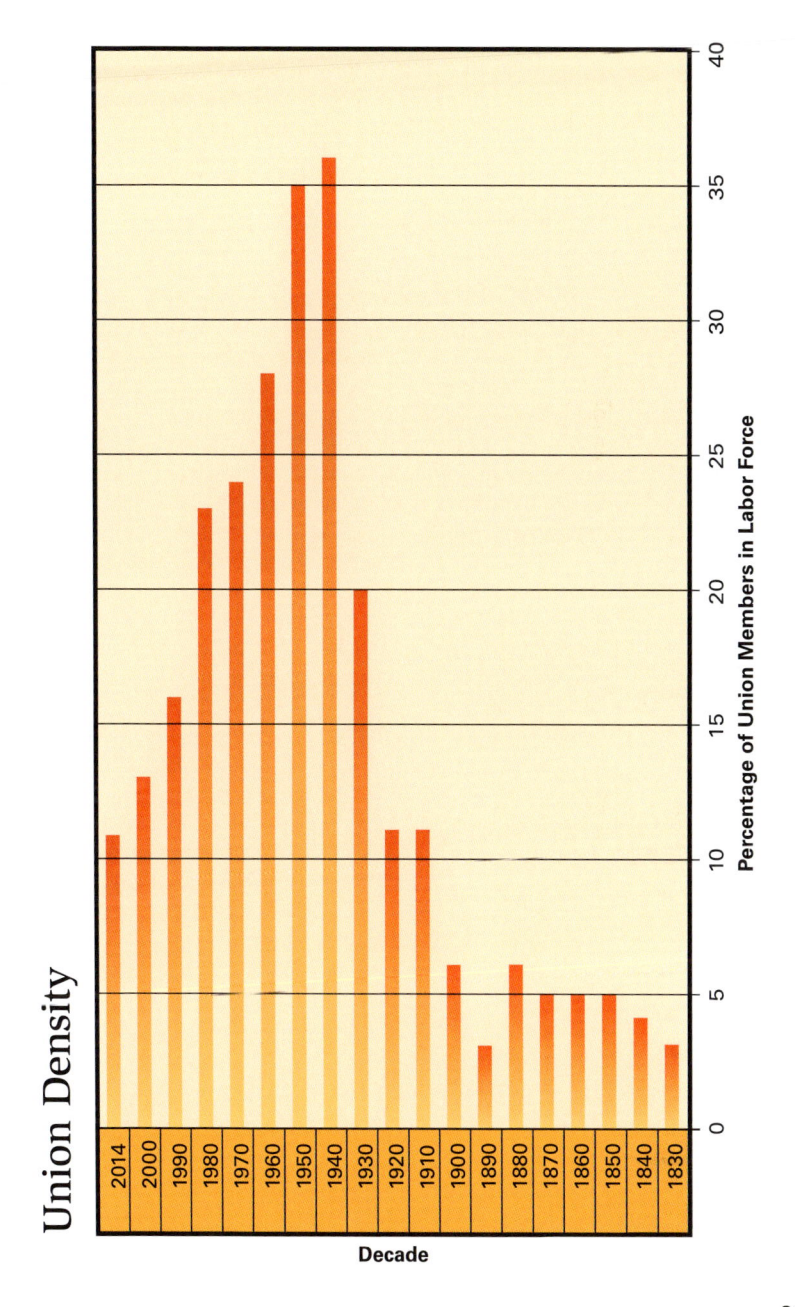

Union Density

Percentage of Union Members in Labor Force vs. **Decade**

Decade	Percentage
2014	~11
2000	~13
1990	~16
1980	~24
1970	~25
1960	~28
1950	~35
1940	~36
1930	~20
1920	~12
1910	~12
1900	~6
1890	~3
1880	~6
1870	~5
1860	~5
1850	~5
1840	~4
1830	~3

AMERICAN LABOR 39

Union Goals and Achievements

Historically, members of the organized labor movement have tried to secure four basic rights.

- To earn "a living wage"
- To work in safe and decent conditions
- To join an organization of their own choosing
- To bargain collectively

After 200 years of battling, bargaining, and striking, unions have achieved their principal goals and more. In 1913, the establishment of the Department of Labor as a cabinet-level department gave the workforce a voice in the government. Union activity led to legislation that set a national minimum wage, a 40-hour workweek, and annual cost-of-living increases and required safety devices and regulations in the workplace. Aggressive collective bargaining resulted in medical insurance plans, pensions, and extra pay for training, vacations, and overtime.

The unions' successes may also contribute to their problems. Many companies have tried to avoid paying the union workers' high wages and expensive benefits by using nonunion employees or offshore workers. In some cases, these practices have resulted in the reduction or elimination of jobs.

Central Labor Councils

You can find out about central labor councils and unions in your area by looking up "Labor Organizations" in your phone book or online.

A *central labor council* is a city or county federation of local unions that are affiliated with various national or international unions. For example, local unions of sheet metal workers, electricians, plumbers and pipe fitters, operating engineers, communications workers, and office and professional employees may all belong to a central labor council. The AFL-CIO has chartered almost 600 central labor councils nationwide.

The principal mission of the central labor council is to mobilize local organizing efforts and political action and to show solidarity for the bargaining demands of specific unions. In addition, the central labor council also coordinates community efforts with local unions to provide training, information, and referral services for workers dealing with financial and personal crises.

Employee Organizations

The National Labor Relations Board defines a *labor organization* as "any organization in which employees participate and which exists for the purpose of dealing with employers concerning grievances, labor disputes, wages, rates of pay, hours of employment, or conditions of work." Labor unions existed before the NLRB was established, so those earlier unions helped shape the definition of a labor organization.

In recent decades, many companies have established employee-participation committees. Sometimes these groups are called by other names such as quality circles and employee-involvement teams. These committees meet regularly with management to discuss employee complaints, productivity, company policies, and other workplace issues. Supporters of these groups suggest that the two-way communication boosts employee morale and encourages the cooperative resolution of workplace problems.

Unions do not favor employee-participation committees because they reduce the need for labor organization. Several unions have challenged these groups by filing unfair labor practice charges with the NLRB, claiming that the employee-participation committees are actually illegal company unions. In certain cases where the NLRB believed that employees were dealing with employers about wages, grievances, and work conditions, the Board ruled that the employee-participation committees were illegal. In other cases, the Board decided that the employee groups were communicating about issues and ruled that they were legal.

Unions already in place probably will continue to challenge the legality of these groups. However, some labor leaders think unions should look at employee participation committees as opportunities to organize from within the company.

Striking Workers Gain Public Support

FEDERAL EMPLOYEES ORDERED BACK TO WORK

Restaurant Chain Charged With Discrimination

Union Files Grievance on Behalf of Teachers

Conflicting Views in the Workplace

Post–World War II prosperity launched the middle class. Millions of Americans earned higher-than-ever wages, received employee benefit packages that included health insurance and pension plans, and bought their first houses and filled them with new appliances and new furniture. All that shopping boosted the economy. Workers trusted their employers and their government. People who had survived the Great Depression and a world war promised to work at their jobs for the next 40 years in exchange for security . . . and a gold watch.

The next generation—the Baby Boomers, born in the years following World War II—expected to have a higher standard of living than their parents. But the economy has since slowed down, companies have laid off employees or cut their benefits, and workers have realized that their retirement is at risk. The children of the Baby Boomers do not have the same optimism about employment opportunities as their parents and grandparents did. For the first time in the history of the American labor movement, young workers do not assume they will have a higher standard of living than their parents.

Every group that has a stake in the economy has different responsibilities and expectations. Often they conflict. When each group understands what others want, it is easier to make and appreciate difficult decisions.

What Workers Want

Most workers, whether or not they belong to a union, share the same concerns and expect the same rights. Employees want a voice in the workplace. Many—even nonunion—wish to speak with a collective voice about broad issues such as job security, wages, hours, fringe benefits, workplace conditions

Conflicting Views in the Workplace

> "Machines don't take sick days or go on strike."
> —*comment from management in response to the complaint that automation and technologies displace workers*

and safety, and a system for resolving problems. When issues relate to personal concerns such as performance appraisals and salaries, training, sexual harassment, discrimination, and unfair treatment, many prefer to speak as individuals.

Employees expect a fair hearing. They want management to listen to the workers with an open mind and to consider that their claims are valid. They also want straight talk. If the company is for sale, employees expect management to share information about terms and conditions so the workers can make appropriate plans about their own employment. If the company plans to outsource jobs, employees want to know if the employer plans to transfer or lay them off. Workers want assurances that they will not be displaced by machinery and technology or replaced by guest workers.

Workers try to strike a balance between keeping their jobs and protecting fringe benefits. These benefits may include

- Seniority (priority status based on length of time the employee has worked for the company)
- Unemployment and disability insurance
- Health care
- Child care and elder care
- Profit sharing and employee stock-option plans
- Continuing education
- Retirement plans (pensions, 401(k)s)
- Workers' compensation (accidental injury, death, or dismemberment insurance)

American workers want democracy in the workplace. However, today's corporate executives may earn many times more than the workers in the same company. Top management often receives bonuses even as workers are laid off. Companies announce record profits after cutting jobs or negotiating employee wage reductions. What workers really want is mutual trust and respect, job security, and a fair share of the profits.

Employee Representatives

When Samuel Gompers, president of the American Federation of Labor, was asked what the labor movement wanted, he said, "More." Representatives for employees—union leaders and negotiators, employee associations, labor lobbyists—have always tried to get more for the workers. "More" ranges from tangible benefits such as wage increases, paid vacations, and matching contributions in retirement funds to intangible government protections in the form of pro-labor legislation, trade restraints, and welfare programs such as Social Security.

Sometimes, however, the representatives have to bargain for less. When a company threatens bankruptcy, workers often have to give back benefits or accept a cut in pay in order to keep their jobs.

What Owners and Management Want

In small companies, the owner is management. In large corporations, the owner is usually a group of investors who have created a legal and financial partnership, joint venture, or syndicate. (For more information, see the *American Business* merit badge pamphlet.) Owners of large companies hire business managers to help them generate a profit.

Unless the top manager or executive is the owner, then everyone in management is a worker with a boss. Management often consists of several levels of administrators.

- Top management includes the chief executive officer and chief financial officer. They determine the goals, objectives, and policies for the company and report directly to the owner.

- Upper management includes top executives who head corporate divisions.

- Middle management executives head departments.

- Lower management directly supervises workers.

Managers at each level have a responsibility to generate profits. Their own job security depends on it. So almost every decision a manager makes—allocating resources, investing in expensive technology, reducing company contributions to employee retirement plans—involves the *bottom line*.

With owners demanding higher profits and employees and labor unions insisting on wage increases and better benefits, management has to make difficult choices. What managers want is the right to manage. Because they have to balance so many special interests with critical financial implications, management expects to have the final authority in the workplace.

Owners

The foremost concern of a company owner (an individual or a group of investors) is to make a profit. How that is accomplished—by gaining a competitive advantage, increasing market share, catering to the customer, improving productivity, or boosting employee morale—is management's concern.

Investment groups own other businesses, too. They make decisions about whether to continue to invest in the companies based on the profitability of those businesses. Just as management may shut down a division in a company to cut costs and improve profitability, the owner may sell an unprofitable company to protect overall profits.

Shareholders

Financial institutions, investment groups, and individuals often buy shares of stock in a company. Each share represents a piece of the company, a percentage of ownership. Some companies offer an employee stock-option plan that allows employees to acquire shares of company stock and receive stock distributions at retirement.

Shareholders want a return on their investment in the company. Most look for a short-term profit, which pressures company management to take short-term action at the expense of long-term goals. Since employee shareholders receive stock distributions at retirement, they are interested in the long-term return on investment.

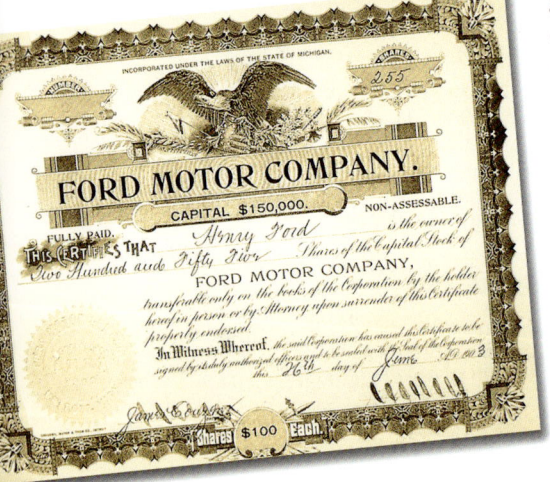

What Others Want

What happens inside a company affects different groups outside the company. Decisions to outsource, raise or lower wages, relocate, or sponsor local community programs influence perceptions and support for the company.

Customers

Customers want to buy quality products and services at the best price. Since customers play a critical role in the success of a business, a company must figure out how to meet consumer needs and still make a profit.

Community

If unemployment is high in a community, citizens want a company to hire local workers. In addition, a community wants a business to fill a niche—to offer a product or service not offered by others—or to offer a better product at a better price than competitors. The community also wants a company to be a good corporate citizen, for example, by sponsoring the arts (such as theater and music groups) or supporting community programs.

Public Officials

The mayor and other public officials want to convince companies that the community is a great place to locate a business because the city benefits from additional tax revenues. If a company is successful, hires local workers, and has a good reputation for the way it handles labor-management relations, then officials can use it as an example to lure other businesses to the community. However, if the company generates negative publicity (from lawsuits, strikes, environmental violations, or workplace injuries), then public officials perceive the company as a problem for the community.

As you can see, these groups have different goals, yet they are linked together. Each time a company addresses an issue in one group, it upsets the balance with other groups. People spend a lot of time at work defending their point of view and insisting on getting what they want. While they are arguing, picketing, or negotiating, they are not making a product, not serving customers or citizens, and not making a profit. When different groups realize that what they have in common (the success of the company) is most important, then they must compromise in areas that are driven by self-interest and make an agreement that best serves everyone.

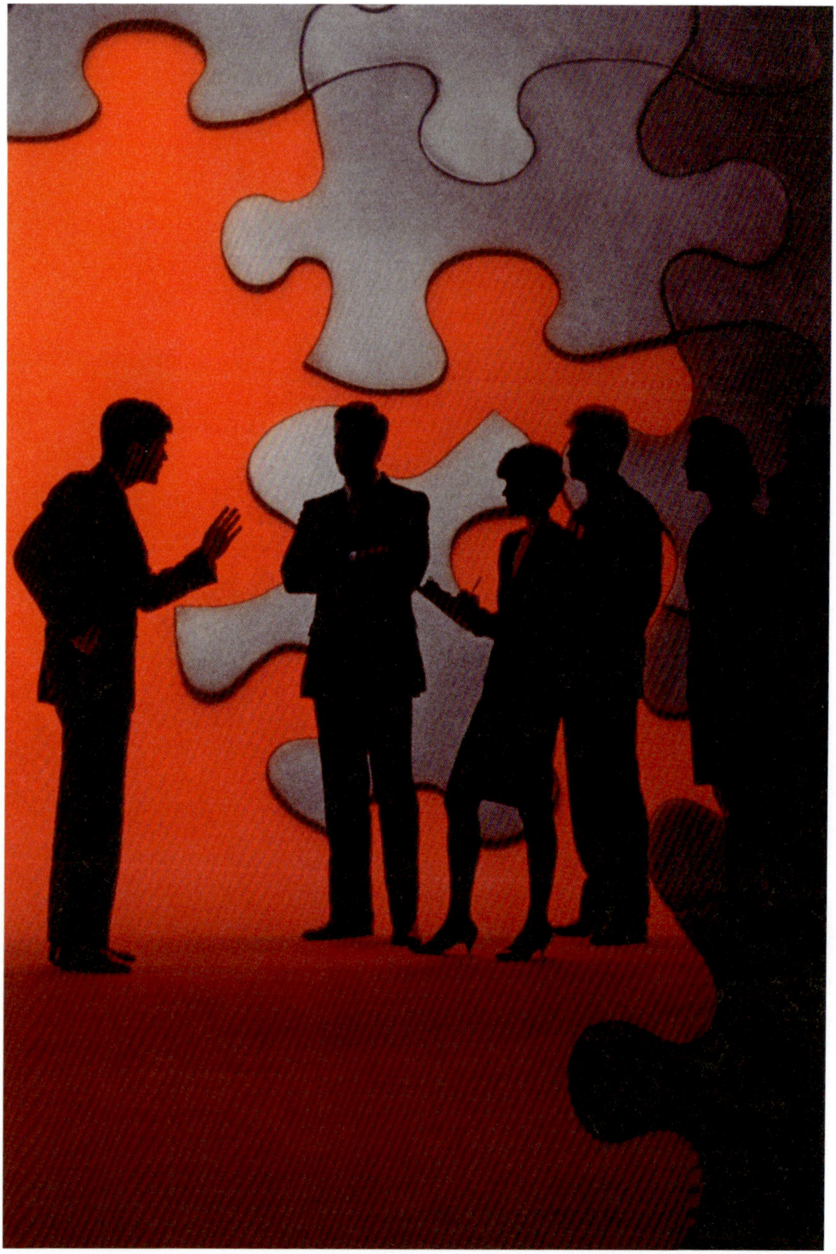

Labor-Management Relations

Suppose that you and two friends started a lawn-care business. Your parent has loaned you all the equipment. All you have to do is maintain it, fuel it, and return it at the end of the summer. You and your friends have agreed to split the profits after paying expenses, and everyone has a plan to spend his share. But today one of your friends broke the edger. Now what?

Did you notice how fast a simple plan becomes complicated? Situations like that happen every day in businesses. Conflicts of interest, if not negotiated, can easily escalate to anger. No wonder workplace relationships get strained.

Laws and Practices That Govern Labor-Management Relations

Labor and management always have had a polarized relationship. The individual employee, working at the whim and mercy of the boss, often feared management. When workers organized, they quickly realized they had some control over their wages and working conditions.

In time, unions took a more aggressive stance with management. Soon, both sides developed an adversarial relationship based on positions, power, and threats. They defined the outcome of collective bargaining as a win for one party, a loss for the other.

Nonunion employees borrowed some of the unions' negotiating techniques but toned them down into a cooperative-bargaining style based on mutual interests. Negotiations—involving individuals or employee groups and management—call for compromises on both sides and a win-win result.

LABOR-MANAGEMENT RELATIONS

Dispute Resolution Continuum →

Cooperative Bargaining Style			Adversarial Model of Collective Bargaining
Conciliation	Mediation	Negotiation	Binding Arbitration
Mutual Interests		Rights	Power
Win-Win			Win-Lose

The political environment influences labor-management disputes. The president (with the consent of the Senate) appoints members to the National Labor Relations Board, which decides cases involving *unfair labor practices* by employers or unions. The appointees generally reflect the pro-labor or antilabor views of the incumbent (current) government officials.

Unfair Labor Practices

The National Labor Relations Act and the Taft-Hartley Act define and prohibit unfair labor practices as practices of discrimination, coercion, and intimidation by management or unions. Employers may not

- Set up company unions.
- Use coercive tactics to discourage union organization.
- Refuse to bargain collectively with unions representing a company's employees.

Unions may not

- Force workers to join organizations *not* of their own choosing.
- Coerce an employee in the selection of a bargaining representative.
- Refuse to bargain in good faith with management.

Collective Bargaining

The negotiation process known as collective bargaining occurs between union and company representatives to discuss wages, hours, working conditions, fringe benefits, and union security. The goal of collective bargaining is to make a contract—a *collective-bargaining agreement*. The contract must meet union needs (and those of nonunion employees covered in the bargaining unit) and employer needs. It also must include specific grievance procedures to resolve labor disputes.

LABOR-MANAGEMENT RELATIONS

Union Grievance Procedure

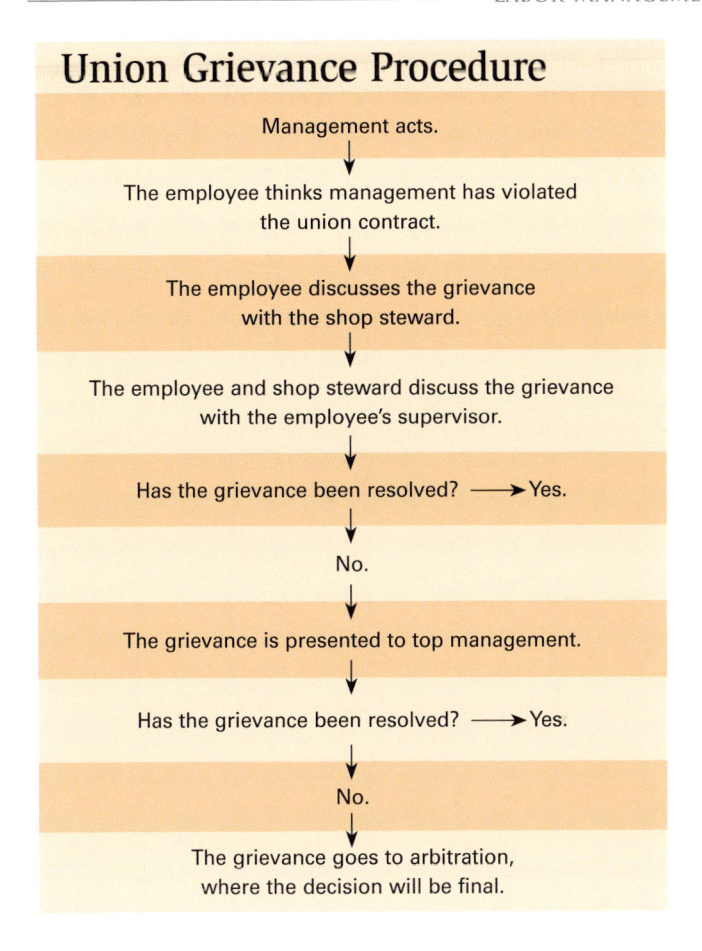

Management acts.
↓
The employee thinks management has violated the union contract.
↓
The employee discusses the grievance with the shop steward.
↓
The employee and shop steward discuss the grievance with the employee's supervisor.
↓
Has the grievance been resolved? ⟶ Yes.
↓
No.
↓
The grievance is presented to top management.
↓
Has the grievance been resolved? ⟶ Yes.
↓
No.
↓
The grievance goes to arbitration, where the decision will be final.

When a contract is about to expire, the union and the company must announce a notice of intent to enter into a collective-bargaining agreement. If the two sides reach an impasse, or fail to agree, then they may call in a neutral third party to mediate a settlement. If the old contract expires before a new one is negotiated and signed, the union may call a strike or the company may call a lockout to pressure the other side to accept terms.

AMERICAN LABOR

LABOR-MANAGEMENT RELATIONS

The law forbids certain public-sector employees from going on strike. Some groups use sick-outs as a form of protest. Firefighters get the "red rash," police catch "blue flu," and teachers suffer from "chalk-dust fever."

A *strike*—the complete cessation of work by employees—is a work stoppage. A *lockout,* in which an employer closes the company and prevents employees from working, is management's version of a strike. Since locked-out workers became eligible for unemployment compensation, the tactic has become less effective than in the past.

Strikes of All Stripes

general strike. A widespread strike of all workers in a geographic area, causing economic paralysis. If successful, the general strike results in a major change in power relations between labor and management.

jurisdictional strike. A work stoppage that results from a dispute between rival unions about which one has the right to represent particular employees. It occurs when rival unions call workers off their jobs to show their strength and support.

organizational strike. An action called to force the employer to recognize the employees' union as their collective-bargaining agent.

sit-down strike. The refusal of striking workers to leave their place of employment in order to prevent other workers from replacing them.

sympathy strike. A walkout by employees—who have no direct grievance against management—in support of workers from another union.

wildcat strike. A work stoppage that occurs when workers leave their jobs (often spontaneously) without the authorization of their union leaders.

Collective bargaining loses its teeth when strikes are prohibited. In those situations, employees use other tactics such as *slowdowns*—deliberate reductions in productivity—and mass absenteeism to pressure employers to meet their demands.

LABOR-MANAGEMENT RELATIONS

Mediation and arbitration of grievances offer cost-effective alternatives to expensive litigation via judicial courts. Both approaches involve using impartial third parties who are committed to confidentiality. *Mediation* is an informal, voluntary negotiation process for resolving disputes. The mediator helps the parties communicate, understand the issues, and reach an agreement but has no decision-making authority. If the parties cannot agree, the dispute goes to *arbitration*, a formal process in which facts and issues are presented to a neutral arbitrator who makes a legally binding decision.

Often, when labor and management have difficulty negotiating an agreement, a mediator will give an opinion about what the final decision might be if the dispute goes to arbitration. That prediction creates an incentive for the parties to reach a settlement before an arbitrator rules against one or the other.

> Work stoppages have been less frequent in the past several decades owing to pro-management arbitration decisions, employers' right to hire replacement strikers, and laws forbidding certain public employees to strike.

Labor-Management Relations

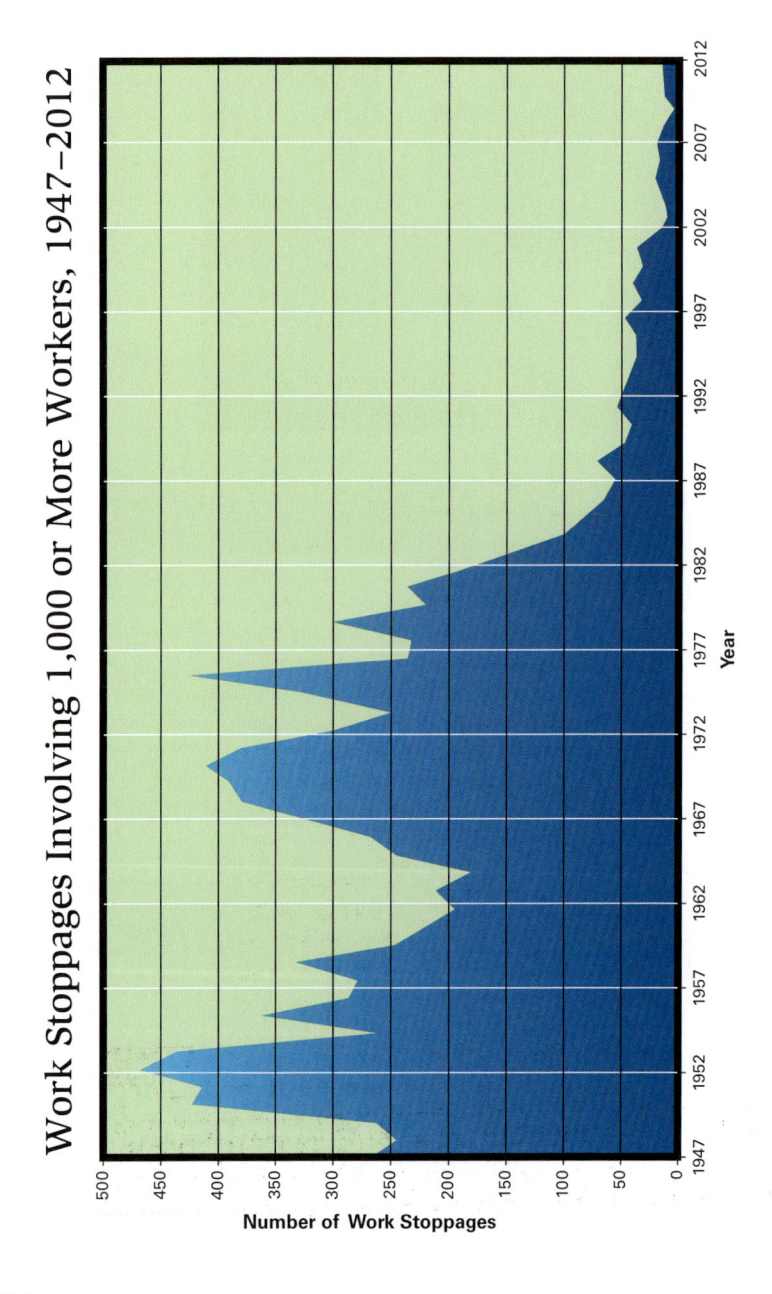

Work Stoppages Involving 1,000 or More Workers, 1947–2012

54   AMERICAN LABOR

Personnel Policies and Procedures

Many nonunion businesses have informal open-door policies to address labor complaints. Workers are encouraged to discuss their concerns with management without fear of any retaliatory actions. Formal internal grievance procedures establish specific steps an employee must take to challenge certain aspects of employment.

Nonunion employees also use mediation and arbitration, as well as *peer review*, which utilizes a panel of the employee's peers to evaluate the dispute and render a decision (which may or may not be binding).

Labor Laws

The rights and responsibilities for labor and management are determined by union contracts and labor legislation.

Hard Hats and Thinking Caps—Two Sides of a Labor Issue

You know by now that the goals of labor and the goals of management often conflict. On any day you can spot newspaper headlines announcing a problem between a union and an employer, a new outsourcing deal, a complaint about the lack of cultural diversity in top management, a discrimination lawsuit, a plant closing, or a threat to slash wages or reduce health insurance benefits. When you start work on requirement 7, pick a current labor issue of widespread interest and then try to understand what caused the problem and what its effect is on labor and on management.

As you prepare to argue the issue (in person or on paper) from different points of view, imagine yourself as the mediator in the labor-management issue you chose. Do not assume one side or the other is right. Be objective and impartial so you can see the facts beneath the issues. Remember: Management's goal is to make a profit. Labor's goal is to make a living wage. Your goal is to defend each party's position within the limits of rights and responsibilities.

Where Now?

Three centuries. Three economic revolutions. It is not business as usual, and it certainly is not labor as usual. The workforce is aging, yet living longer than earlier generations. Baby Boomers are either not willing to retire in their 60s or not financially prepared to retire. Older workers are holding on to positions that younger workers expected to fill.

Globalization has changed the way Americans conduct business *and* the way people work. Outsourcing has moved both blue-collar and white-collar jobs out of the United States. Opportunities in fields such as computer science are no longer plentiful, although experts predict that there will be plenty of face-to-face positions that cannot be moved overseas. Millions of positions for unskilled and semiskilled workers in food service and retail sales occupations will be available, yet many unemployed skilled workers will compete for those low-paying jobs. The American labor movement faces a lot of knotty problems and challenges, but it is not at the end of its rope.

Labor Laws

Anti-Trust Act of 1914 (Clayton Act). This pro-labor law states that union activities are not illegal and limits the courts' jurisdiction to issue injunctions against labor organizations.

Railway Labor Act of 1926. This pro-labor act protects the collective-bargaining rights of interstate railway employees (amended in 1934 to include airlines). This law established the National Railroad Adjustment Board to arbitrate grievances that arise from labor-management contracts.

Davis-Bacon Act of 1931. A pro-labor law that requires contractors on federal government construction projects to pay the prevailing rates and fringe benefits.

Norris-LaGuardia Act of 1932. This pro-labor act outlawed the *yellow-dog contract*—a statement workers sometimes were forced to sign in which they promised that they would *not* join a union. In addition, this law limits the power of federal courts to issue injunctions against union activity in labor disputes.

National Labor Relations Act of 1935 (Wagner Act). A pro-labor law that applies to all companies and employees in activities affecting interstate commerce except for agricultural laborers, government employees, and people covered by the Railway Labor Act. It established

LABOR-MANAGEMENT RELATIONS

a National Labor Relations Board to safeguard workers' rights to organize unions and bargain collectively through representatives of their own choosing.

Anti-Strikebreaker Act of 1936 (Byrnes Act). This pro-labor law, which was amended in 1938, prohibits employers from transporting people across state lines to break strikes or threaten organizing or bargaining efforts.

Walsh-Healy Public Contracts Act of 1936. A pro-labor act that established basic labor standards for work performed on U.S. government contracts, including minimum wages, overtime compensation, prohibitions against hiring convicts and children under 18, and requirements related to health and safety.

Fair Labor Standards Act of 1938 (Wages and Hours Act). This pro-labor law, amended in 1949, 1955, 1961, 1963, 1966, and 1996, established minimum hourly wages and overtime payments for all workers in covered businesses involving interstate commerce. This law requires that men and women performing equal work be paid equal wages and regulates the employment of children under age 18.

Labor-Management Relations Act of 1947 (Taft-Hartley Act). An antilabor law that allows states to enact right-to-work laws. It prohibits closed shops and restricts the activities and power of labor unions.

Labor-Management Reporting and Disclosure Act of 1959 (Landrum-Griffin Act). This law, prompted by investigations into racketeering charges and intended to protect union members from corrupt leaders, includes regulations for union election procedures and government supervision of unions' financial affairs.

Civil Rights Act of 1964. This law prohibits unions, employers, and employment agencies from discriminating against workers or clients based on race, color, sex, religion, or national origin. This law established the Equal Employment Opportunity Commission to handle complaints about violations of this act. Its provisions were extended to public-sector employers in 1972.

Occupational Safety Health Act of 1970. This pro-labor law authorizes the secretary of labor to establish and enforce health and safety standards in workplaces.

Career Opportunities in Labor Relations

The field of labor relations includes all the interactions between a company's management and organized labor or nonunion employees. Careers range from recruiters to employee benefits specialists to administrative law judges.

Many unions today are hiring staff employees in a number of positions, such as IT technicians, researchers, economists, teachers and educators, field organizers, legislative aides, clerical workers, and other areas. Young people who feel a commitment to serving working people are particularly welcomed by labor organizations.

There are also opportunities to work in nonprofit organizations, such as those that serve low-income families and have social justice aims. The experience gained in these organizations is particularly worthwhile because young workers are often immediately put into positions that require resourcefulness, imagination, and leadership.

Human Resources

This area concerns all aspects involving the employees of a company, including hiring, paying, training, and discharging personnel as well as helping to develop policies.

A *human resources generalist* handles the full range of responsibilities relating to personnel. In a large corporation, a *director of human resources* develops and coordinates personnel policies and procedures and oversees the following departments, which are headed by experienced managers:

Career Opportunities in Labor Relations

Employment. An *employment and placement manager* handles the hiring and separation (leaving the company) of employees and supervises the people in the following positions.

- A *recruiter* often travels to find and interview promising job candidates. The recruiter must understand the company and its policies, as well as employment laws, in order to discuss wages, working conditions, and opportunities.

- An *equal employment opportunity officer, representative,* or *affirmative action coordinator* works in a large corporation, handles discrimination grievances, and makes sure that company practices are not in violation of the law.

Compensation. A *compensation manager* sets up and maintains the company's pay system and compares the pay rates to other companies to ensure that the pay scale complies with legal regulations. The manager makes compensation decisions based on information from people in the following positions:

- A *job analysis specialist* collects and studies information about job duties to classify positions and develop job descriptions.

- An *occupational analyst* studies the effects of industry and occupational trends on worker relationships and often acts as a technical link between the company and other organizations.

Benefits. An *employee benefits manager* handles the company's benefits program, which includes insurance (health, disability, life, accidental death and dismemberment) and pension plans (savings, profit sharing, stock ownership). A benefits manager (and benefits specialist) must know the current laws and regulations that affect employee benefits. An *employee assistance plan manager,* or *employee welfare manager,* is responsible for pro grams that help employees balance their work and personal lives such as those relating to child care, elder care, transportation and carpooling, physical fitness, and counseling.

Training and Development. A *training and development manager* is responsible for programs to develop employees' skills, improve productivity and quality of work, and boost morale. A *training specialist* plans and directs activities that include on-the-job training for new employees, new skills training in response to technological changes, and executive development programs.

Industrial Relations

A *director of industrial relations* makes labor policy and collaborates with the director of human resources and other managers about personnel policies that affect unionized employees. The director negotiates collective-bargaining agreements and coordinates grievance procedures. A *labor-relations manager* is responsible for implementing industrial labor-relations programs, overseeing the preparation of information for negotiating collective-bargaining agreements, and administering union contracts. The position requires extensive knowledge about labor law and collective-bargaining trends.

Dispute Resolution

This negotiation process for settling disputes is an alternative to litigation. Resolutions at this level save much time and money, so third-party individuals should be knowledgeable and experienced in the areas of labor law and industrial relations.

- A *conciliator* assumes the responsibility for keeping disputing parties in negotiations until they reach a voluntary settlement. As a third party, the conciliator tries to establish communication between disputants and build the trust necessary for a cooperative solution.

- A *mediator* is an impartial third party who is appointed to help resolve a labor-management dispute. The mediator advises, but has no decision-making authority. An *arbitrator* is an impartial individual who conducts a formal hearing about a labor-management dispute and renders a decision that may or may not be binding on both sides.

- An *administrative law judge* decides cases that cannot be resolved through mediation or arbitration or are so complex and critical that they go directly to court.

Qualifications, Education, and Training

Entry-level careers in human resources and industrial labor relations generally require a college education with majors in human resources, personnel administration, or industrial and labor relations. A combination of interdisciplinary courses in the social sciences, business, and behavioral sciences plus courses in computers and information systems provide a strong base of knowledge. Candidates with experience from internships or work-study programs have an edge over applicants with no work experience.

For certain specialties such as employment benefits, industrial relations, and dispute resolution, a background in law is necessary. Many labor-relations positions require graduate study. Management positions demand advanced degrees in human resources, labor relations, or business administration.

Human resources workers and labor-relations specialists need good people skills to interact effectively with a culturally diverse workforce. Like dispute-resolution specialists, they should demonstrate the qualities of fair-mindedness, discretion, and compassion as well as the abilities to analyze problems, interpret statistics, function under pressure, and manage conflicting points of view.

A federal administrative law judge must have experience as a lawyer and pass a competitive examination administered by the U.S. Office of Personnel Management. The judge is appointed (for life) to the bench by one of several federal agencies and then receives judicial training from an organization such as the American Bar Association.

Many conciliators, mediators, and arbitrators have law degrees with a specialization in conflict management. Those affiliated with mediation organizations must complete a training course and an apprenticeship and agree to uphold certain ethical standards.

If you are interested in pursuing one of these careers, consider a summer internship in a personnel or human resources department. You will get on-the-job training in basic administrative duties and gain an appreciation for the field of labor relations.

Labor-Related Resources

Scouting Literature
American Business, Citizenship in the Nation, Citizenship in the World, Communication, Entrepreneurship, Law, Public Speaking, and *Salesmanship* merit badge pamphlets

> Visit the Boy Scouts of America's official retail website at www.scoutshop.org (with your parent's permission) for a complete listing of all merit badge pamphlets and other helpful Scouting materials and supplies.

Books
Bartoletti, Susan Campbell. *Kids on Strike.* HMH Books for Young Readers, 2003.

Dubofsky, Melvyn, and Foster R. Dulles. *Labor in America: A History.* Wiley-Blackwell, 2010.

Freedman, Russell. *Kids at Work: Lewis Hine and the Crusade Against Child Labor.* HMH Books for Young Readers, 1998.

Le Blanc, Paul. *A Short History of the U.S. Working Class: From Colonial Times to the Twenty-First Century.* Humanity Books, 1999.

Lichtenstein, Nelson. *State of the Union: A Century of American Labor.* Princeton University Press, 2013.

Murray, R. Emmett. *Lexicon of Labor: More Than 500 Key Terms, Biographical Sketches, and Historical Insights Concerning Labor in America.* The New Press, 2010.

Ross, Stewart. *The Industrial Revolution: Documenting History.* Franklin Watts, 2001.

Stein, R. Conrad. *The Pullman Strike and the Labor Movement in American History.* Enslow Publishers, 2001.

U.S. Department of Labor. *Occupational Outlook Handbook (current year).* Skyhorse Publishing, 2014.

Woodburn, Judith. *A Multicultural Portrait of Labor in America.* Benchmark Books, 1994.

Zaniello, Tom. *Working Stiffs, Union Maids, Reds, and Riffraff: An Expanded Guide to Films About Labor.* ILR Press, 2003.

Biographies About American Labor Leaders

Collins, David R. *Farmworker's Friend: The Story of Cesar Chavez.* Carolrhoda Books, 1996.

Josephson, Judith Pinkerton. *Mother Jones: Fierce Fighter for Workers' Rights.* Lerner Publications, 1996.

Lichtenstein, Nathan. *Walter Reuther: The Most Dangerous Man in Detroit.* University of Illinois Press, 1997.

Reef, Catherine. *A. Philip Randolph: Union Leader and Civil Rights Crusader.* Enslow Publishers, 2001.

Streissguth, Thomas. *Legendary Labor Leaders.* Oliver Press Inc., 1998.

Organizations and Websites

American Arbitration Association
120 Broadway, Floor 21
New York, NY 10271
Telephone: 212-716-5800
Website: www.adr.org

American Federation of Labor and Congress of Industrial Organizations
815 16th St. NW
Washington, DC 20006
Telephone: 202-637-5000
Website: https://aflcio.org/

American Labor Studies Center
16 Birchwood Court
Loudonville, NY 12211-2057
Telephone: 518-331-4474
Website: www.labor-studies.org

Illinois Labor History Society
430 S. Michigan Ave, Room WB 1806
Chicago, IL 60605
Telephone: 312-341-2247
Website: www.illinoislaborhistory.org

Labor Heritage Foundation
815 16th St. NW
Washington, DC 20006
Telephone: 202-639-6204
Website: www.laborheritage.org

LaborStart
Website: www.laborstart.org/usa

National Labor Relations Board
1015 Half St. SE
Washington, D.C. 20570-0001
Toll-free telephone: 844-762-6572
Website: www.nlrb.gov

Occupational Safety and Health Administration
200 Constitution Ave. NW
Room N3626
Washington, DC 20210
Toll-free telephone: 800-321-6742
Website: www.osha.gov

U.S. Bureau of Labor Statistics
Postal Square Building
2 Massachusetts Ave. NE
Washington, DC 20212-0001
Telephone: 202-691-5200
Website: www.bls.gov

U.S. Department of Labor
200 Constitution Ave. NW
Washington, DC 20210
Toll-free telephone: 866-487-2365
Website: www.dol.gov

Wisconsin Labor History Society
6333 W. Bluemound Road
Milwaukee WI 53213
Telephone: 414-771-0700
Website: www.wisconsinlaborhistory.org

Labor-Related Resources

Acknowledgments

We are appreciative of the support from the following individuals on this update of the *American Labor* merit badge pamphlet:
- Kenneth A. Germanson, president emeritus, Wisconsin Labor History Society
- Paul Cole, executive director, American Labor Studies Center
- David Newby, retired president, Wisconsin AFL-CIO
- Evelyn Hershey, education director, American Labor Museum

For their past support, the Boy Scouts of America thanks Dr. George Green, professor of history at the University of Texas at Arlington, for his guidance about the significant events in the history of the American labor movement, and the Tarrant County Central Labor Council for its openness and support.

The Boy Scouts of America is grateful to the men and women serving on the National Merit [...] for the impr[...] this pamph[...]

Photo a[...]

Ford Motor[...] page 4[...]

Internatio[...] archiv[...]

Kheel Cen[...] Docum[...] courte[...]

Library of[...] Photo[...] pages[...] and 2[...]

National Archives and Records Administration, courtesy—pages 10 and 13

National Photo Company Collection, Library of Congress, courtesy—page 11

Shutterstock.com—
cover (*welding mask*, ©Theerapol Pongkangsananan; *pilot's cap*, ©Moises Fernandez Acosta; *picket illustration*, ©J.D.S; *flag*, ©Alex Kosev; *construction gear*, ©indigolotos; *clapper board*, ©Andrey_Kuzmin); pages 6 (*background*, ©Edward Bruns; *group*, ©Blend Images; *business team*, ©Stephen Coburn; *parcel delivery*, ©kurhan), 23 (©nmedia), 24 (©egd), 27 (©craig hill), 28 (*remote*, ©Stockforlife; *DVD*, ©MadTatyana), 32 (*background*, ©wavebreakmedia; *group*, ©Rawpixel; *construction site*, ©Blend Images), 33 (©Alina Vasilescu), 37 (©Pressmaster), 38 (©Rob Byron), 42 (*background*, ©Dan Thornberg), 48 (©Steve Cukrov), and

[...]rtesy—

[...]sie the

[...] not [...]ty [...]couts

64